INSPIRATION POINT

by

Michael R. Helgens & Kevin Brubaker

"You can't wait for inspiration. You have to go after it with a club." ~Jack London

Copyright:
Michael R. Helgens and Kevin Brubaker

For rights to produce contact:
Michael R. Helgens
1612 C Avenue NE
Cedar Rapids, IA 52402
319-821-0682
michael.helgens@gmail.com

This text or any portion thereof may not be reproduced or used in any manner whatsoever without the express written permission of the publisher or authors except for the use of brief quotations in a review.

Printed in the United States of America

First Printing, 2013

Published by:
Media Adventures, LLC
2925 Schultz Drive NW
Cedar Rapids, IA 52402
www.jumpstartmovie.com

You can listen to the radio broadcast version of Inspiration Point at
http://www.StrobieStudios.com

Copyright © 2013 Michael R. Helgens & Kevin Brubaker
All rights reserved.
ISBN: 0615877966
ISBN-13: 978-0615877969

Cast of Characters

Nemo Tumblety:	A young man 20-30 years old
Dr. Raphael Alexander:	A male psychiatrist 30-50 years old
Sergeant Peter Conner:	A prison employee 20-30 years old
Fred Abberline:	A private investigator 25-50 years old
Hugo Jamison:	An older man and the first victim 35-45 years old
Harriet Tubbs:	A very old woman and the second victim 45-65 years old
Arden Hetzler:	A man about Nemo's age and the third victim 20-30 years old
Roland Tarrance:	The bartender and accomplice 20-25 years old
Mrs. Tabitha Conner:	Sergeant Conner's wife 20-30 years old
Seamus Drinn:	Inspiration Point's new bartender 35-55 years old.

Scene

A psychiatrist's office, a comfortable bar and a kill room.

ACT I

> (NEMO sits on the sofa in RAPHAEL'S office while RAPHAEL sits behind a desk.)

NEMO

The thing that lets me feel like I'm the only person in control is the moment when you watch the light go out in someone's eyes. Up until that moment they have so much fight in them and they'll do anything to survive. When you've shown them that they can only surrender...
(sigh)
...and then they do and they're gone. It doesn't ever last long enough. You know what I mean, doc?

DR. ALEXANDER

If I'm to help you, you need to answer my questions and you've been evasive, at best, Mr. Tumblety.

NEMO

Call me Nemo. You're the only person who really talks to me anymore apart from Officer Conners. It's nice to hear your own name once in a while.

DR. ALEXANDER

Mr. Tumblety, I am a doctor, and you are my patient. I think it best that we maintain a professional relationship.

NEMO

I guess that's OK, for now.

DR. ALEXANDER

Again, Mr. Tumblety, answer the question—when did all of this begin?

NEMO

Sure. I guess my work started with the first cut.

DR. ALEXANDER

And when was that?

NEMO

You always remember your first. His name was Jamison, Hugo Jamison. No one says Hugo's name very much anymore. That's why I picked him.

DR. ALEXANDER

You had a plan?

NEMO

People don't get it.

DR. ALEXANDER
    What's that?

NEMO
    They aren't really free.

DR. ALEXANDER
    You were trying to help people?

NEMO
    That's right, but you can't just walk up to a person and tell them that they're a slave—they'll just laugh you out of the room and then go back to paying the bills and showing up to work on time every day...disgusting!

DR. ALEXANDER
    So why did you select Mr. Jamison?

NEMO
    I met him at a bar. The poor guy was really down on his luck. Turns out he'd been keeping a lot of secrets.

DR. ALEXANDER
    A lot of people are in his position. Why was he so special?

NEMO
    No one cared about the guy. His so called friends and family just used him and kept putting him further behind.

DR. ALEXANDER
    You chose him because no one would miss him.

NEMO
    Yeah, and I was right. I'm pretty sure, until I told the police where to find him, no one had even tried looking for him.

DR. ALEXANDER
    Tell me what happened with Mr. Jamison.

NEMO
    Everything?

DR. ALEXANDER
    Yes.

NEMO
    If you say so, but remember...you asked for it.

DR. ALEXANDER
    Proceed, Mr. Tumblety.

NEMO
    I was at home thinking about life and what I wanted to do with mine. I looked online, but nothing really inspired me so I decided to go to Inspiration Point.

DR. ALEXANDER
    I've heard of it.

NEMO
    It's run down, but the people are nice and it's always a good time. I opened the door and the first thing that hit me was the music.

> *(The lights dim in RAPHAEL'S office and come up on the bar. ROLAND is behind the bar and HUGO is sitting at a table drinking a beer. NEMO gets up and goes to the bar. Funeral music begins to play when he opens the door.)*

ROLAND
    (Eager to please)
    What'll you have, Nemo?

NEMO
    Gimme some Jack.

ROLAND
    Sure thing.
        (ROLAND pours a drink and gives it to NEMO)
    Here you go.

NEMO
    Did someone die?

ROLAND
    Probably.

NEMO
    I mean the music.

ROLAND
    Oh, that? We got one of those Internet jukeboxes and that guy over there on his eighth beer keeps playing the stuff.

NEMO
    I'll go talk with him. Maybe I can help him out.

ROLAND
	Be my guest. You wanna start a tab?

NEMO
	No, I'm not staying long.

		(ROLAND shakes his head and smiles knowingly while
		NEMO focuses his attention on HUGO and walks to
		his table.)

NEMO
	This seat taken?

HUGO JAMISON
	No, but you'll probably have a better time with someone else.

NEMO
	Sure, I could go, but it seems like you could use a sympathetic ear.
			(NEMO sits)
	Tell me what's wrong.

HUGO
	Well, I'm broke and I don't have anyone to come home to at night. Every time I think that I might be able to start to get ahead of the game something else happens that makes things worse. In short...

		(The lights go down in the bar during HUGO'S
		speech and back up in RAPHAEL'S office at the end.
		NEMO returns to the sofa to address RAPHAEL.
		During this moment HUGO moves to the kill room and
		is strapped to NEMO'S table.)

NEMO
	...the guy's life was a mess. My new friend Hugo was a prisoner and he didn't even know it. I asked him if he wanted to join me for something a little heavier than drinking to help him forget all of his troubles and he agreed to come home with me. After he passed out I tied him up and spent the evening thinking about the fun we were about to have.

		(NEMO gets up and the lights go down in RAPHAEL'S
		office while coming up on NEMO'S kill room. NEMO
		splashes HUGO with a glass of water.)

HUGO
			(Spluttering)
	What the hell?

NEMO

    Sorry to wake you so early, but I haven't really slept and I couldn't wait any longer.

HUGO

    Who are you?

NEMO

    Don't you remember me? We spent the whole night together. Go on, think back.

HUGO

    You were at the bar. What's going on?

NEMO

    I'm here to help set you free.

HUGO

    What do you mean free? Whatever I told you—it's not as bad as you think. I can handle it.

NEMO

    (Calm and soothing)
    Enough, you are not handling it, Hugo. You're falling apart and what's worse...you know that you're not going to succeed, but you keep trying.

HUGO

    Listen, if you need money...

NEMO

    Hugo, you already told me that you don't have any. You need to see that I want to help you. Don't you understand that money, your job, the thing that you call a life is just designed to make you a slave?

HUGO

    There's nothing I can do about it, man, it's just the way things are. I'm fine. Just untie me, I'll leave and no one has to know about any of this.

NEMO

    No, Hugo, you don't understand, but you will.

HUGO

    I'm begging you.

NEMO

    No one, but me, cares about you, Hugo, you said so yourself. You're trapped in a life that you can't fix. Tell me that I'm wrong and I'll let you go.

HUGO
(Distraught)
You're wrong!

NEMO

I'm afraid that was unconvincing. Listen, Let me show you. You just have to see that you are powerless. Then, when you ask me for your freedom, I'll give it to you.

(The lights go down on NEMO'S kill room and come back up on RAPHAEL'S office. While NEMO talks to RAPHAEL tourniquets are added to HUGO'S wrists and ankles to stop blood loss and a saw (powered or otherwise) is added to the table. Two of Hugo's fingers are "removed".)

DR. ALEXANDER

Did he ask for his freedom?

NEMO

Who's telling the story here, Raph, you're messing up my narrative flow.

DR. ALEXANDER

Fine, proceed.

NEMO

I guess this is a good spot for an interlude, anyway. You're a pretty wealthy guy, right, Dr. Alexander?

DR. ALEXANDER

We're not talking about me. What does that have to do with anything?

NEMO

Have you ever been poor?

DR. ALEXANDER

Mr. Tumblety, I don't see how that is relevant.

NEMO

I'm gonna guess no, so you've probably never really done a lot of butcher work.

DR. ALEXANDER

No.

NEMO

But I'm sure you've cooked up a few steaks.

DR. ALEXANDER

Of course.

NEMO
That's why I was so sure that it would be like cutting into a fresh steak, but I was wrong.
> (NEMO sits forward and slowly cuts through an invisible "fruit")

The first time you cut into a person it's more like pushing a knife into a cantaloupe. A little tough at first, but once you get going it gets easier and before you know it, with a little tearing and ripping, you're all the way through.

DR. ALEXANDER
I see.

NEMO
I used the knife that I spent the night sharpening to take off two of Hugo's fingers. He screamed for a long time, but he eventually calmed down enough for us to talk.

> *(The lights come back up in NEMO'S kill room and he returns from the office.)*

NEMO
So this is what it's like, Hugo. No matter what, life takes things from you and you can't get them back.

HUGO
If you are going to kill me just do it already.

NEMO
I'm not going to kill you; I'm going to set you free.

HUGO
What's the difference?

NEMO
You'll know. Your whole life has led you to this moment. You've already lost so much, but you'll have to lose more before you are ready. Taking off your fingers was a bit more difficult than I thought it would be so I brought this to help us.

> *(NEMO dons rubber gloves and switches on a CD player. The lights go down and either the power saw noise or a handsaw cutting through a piece of particularly juicy fruit, screaming and violin music are all the audience hears. When the lights come back up HUGO'S hands and feet have been removed and there is a great deal of blood on both him and NEMO. NEMO splashes HUGO with another cup of water.)*

NEMO

    So that's it, Hugo. No more excuses, nothing left to make you a slave.

HUGO

    (Whispering)
    I want to die.

NEMO

    (Upset)
    No, no, no...that is not what this is about. You are not dying you are escaping.

HUGO

    I...I want to be set free.

NEMO

    (Moves closer)
    What was that?

    (HUGO groans and NEMO rushes close to him.)

NEMO

    No, you can't go yet. I need you, Hugo. Please (slapping his face), come on, not yet.

HUGO

    Nemo.

NEMO

    Yes, Hugo?

HUGO

    I want...I want you to set me free...

NEMO

    Oh, my friend, that is wonderful. I'm so happy for you. Here, you don't have to worry any more. (Nemo slowly plunges a knife into Hugo's chest while delivering the next line) Shhhh...there you go. You sleep now.

    (NEMO walks back to the doctor's office, removes his gloves and tosses them in the trash by DR. ALEXANDER'S desk before taking his place on the sofa.)

DR. ALEXANDER

    (sets down his notepad)
    Nemo, that was very disturbing.

NEMO

    Look I tried to warn you, but now that you know isn't it liberating?

DR. ALEXANDER
There is no need for us to continue these
conversations. I have what I need for my evaluation.

NEMO
No. Everything I've done so far has been so that you
could meet me. We have to talk until you understand my
work.

DR. ALEXANDER
Mr. Tumblety I have other patients to see today so
let's get to the point. What is there left for me to
understand?

NEMO
Well, it's just, no...I promised myself that we would
make it through this the right way.

DR. ALEXANDER
What do you mean?

NEMO
Look, I didn't want to tell you this yet, but I can see
that if I don't, you'll jump ship so here goes. I met
this girl and she's really nice. The trouble is, she
can't really speak now that she doesn't have hands.

DR. ALEXANDER
What do you mean?

NEMO
(Nemo signs to the doctor "You speak
sign language." while speaking)
Well, it's just I heard that you speak sign language
too, don't you?

DR. ALEXANDER
Yes?

NEMO
Right, and when I met Alexi we had fantastic
conversations, but now she just sits there saying
nothing.

DR. ALEXANDER
(Upset)
You cannot seriously expect me to believe that you have
my daughter somewhere. We just got a letter from her
two days ago and you've been in prison for nearly a
month.

NEMO
    Yeah, I asked a friend of mine to wait until after the trial to mail it. Shall I recite a few lines for you?

DR. ALEXANDER
        (Defeated)
    What do you want?

NEMO
    I want to help set your daughter free, but she can't ask me to help her any more since I took her hands and that doesn't really work for me so I need you to ask for her.

DR. ALEXANDER
    I'll not do it.

NEMO
    I think this session is over, doc.

DR. ALEXANDER
    You tell me where she is this instant or so help me I'll...

NEMO
    Listen, doc, if you end our relationship I'll just have to have my friend stop caring for your daughter. If we get to talk, then maybe we can work something out. So, what do you say, same time tomorrow?

        (NEMO leaves the office and is escorted away by SERGEANT CONNOR who has been waiting outside the door. RAPHAEL buries his head in his hands, looks up when the door closes and then picks up the phone. The lights go down in the office.)

ACT II

(We show that the next day has arrived and the lights come back up in RAPHAEL'S office. SERGEANT CONNOR escorts NEMO back to the door and NEMO enters cheerful. He takes his place on the sofa.)

NEMO

    Hey, doc, how're you feeling?

DR. ALEXANDER

        (Forced politeness)
    Mr. Tumblety, I...

NEMO

    Doc, I think we can be on a first name basis at this point, don't you?

DR. ALEXANDER

    Fine, Nemo, I want you to let my daughter go.

NEMO

        (Hopeful)
    You mean set her free?

DR. ALEXANDER

    No, I need to know she's alive.

NEMO

    I'm not really sure I can help with that.

DR. ALEXANDER

    If you want me to listen to you, you have to give me something.

NEMO

    Tell you what, since I need you focused, I'll see what I can work out before our next talk.

DR. ALEXANDER

    Perfect.

NEMO

    So, Raphael, are you ready for more?

DR. ALEXANDER

    If you will not tell me where Alexi is then I really have no choice.

NEMO

    Sure you do, Raph, you can choose freedom for Alexi or you can learn more about my calling.

DR. ALEXANDER
    I can't do this.

NEMO
    What's that?

DR. ALEXANDER
    I can't sit here and pretend to have a normal
    conversation with you while you are holding Alexi.

NEMO
    This is important.

DR. ALEXANDER
    Nemo, Sergeant Conner is waiting in the reception area
    to take you back to your cell. Please, just go.

NEMO
    But our hour isn't even up yet.

DR. ALEXANDER
    If I cannot convince you to release my daughter then we
    have nothing more to discuss.

NEMO
    Are you sure? Think about it for just a minute before
    you answer. If you send me away then you're giving
    Alexi to me.

DR. ALEXANDER
    My only solace is that you are in prison, Mr. Tumblety.
    That will make it more difficult for you to finish...
    what did you call it? Your "work".

NEMO
    Alright. I had really hoped this would go differently.

DR. ALEXANDER
            (Resigned)
    So did I.

        (NEMO gets up and walks to the door and RAPHAEL
        follows close behind, but doesn't leave the office
        while he addresses SERGEANT CONNOR.)

SERGEANT PETER CONNER
    Done already?

DR. ALEXANDER
    Mr. Tumblety needs to go back to his cell now. Nemo,
    you can come back when you can show me what you
    promised.

NEMO
    Ah, sure thing. See you tomorrow.

SERGEANT CONNER
    C'mon, Nemo, let's go.

    (While NEMO and SERGEANT CONNOR talk they walk around the theatre until near the end of their conversation when NEMO is taken to a seat among the audience which is his cell. At the proper time the cell door can be heard closing.)

NEMO
    You know, Pete, that's something I've never done.

SERGEANT CONNER
    What's that?

NEMO
    Helped a child to know freedom.

SERGEANT CONNER
    Come on, Nemo, you know I don't like it when you talk like that.

NEMO
    I know, but children are already so free. I could save them before they ever have the chance to know the life of a slave. That'd be real nice.

SERGEANT CONNER
    (Unconvinced)
    Sure.

NEMO
    I'm glad you agree. So listen. I was wondering if you could help me with something.

SERGEANT CONNER
    What's that?

NEMO
    My girlfriend promised to send me a box of cookies and I'd really prefer they weren't handled by a bunch of people.

SERGEANT CONNER
    Why do you think I can help with that?

NEMO
    I've heard from some of the other guys that you're a man who can get things through "unmolested"—pictures of their girls, unopened private letters, stuff like that.

SERGEANT CONNER
    So you'd like your cookies to be free of outside
    influences, as it were.

NEMO
    And I realize that you do this particular brand of work
    at great personal risk to yourself, so I'd be willing
    to make sure that you get to have some.

SERGEANT CONNER
    It's going to take more than a cookie, but that's a
    start.

NEMO
    So I should have my girlfriend put in a little extra
    for you?

SERGEANT CONNER
    Yeah, let's say 50 cookies and I'll make sure that you
    get first dibs on your baked goods.

NEMO
    OK, can you just put your phone on speaker and dial it
    for me.

SERGEANT CONNER
    Better make it 70 cookies if I gotta help you make the
    call too.

NEMO
    Deal.

SERGEANT CONNER
    What's the number?

NEMO
    324-4775

        (SERGEANT CONNOR dials the number and hold the
        phone out for NEMO to talk. ROLAND answers the
        phone at the bar.)

ROLAND
    Hello?

NEMO
    Hey, it's Nemo.

ROLAND
    Oh, uh, yeah, what's up?

NEMO
    Tell Tonya to put 70 bucks in with the cookies that she's going to drop off for me at the prison today. Can you do that?

ROLAND
    70 bucks and some cookies. Yeah, I can manage that.

NEMO
    Good. Tell her I'll pay her back when I can.

ROLAND
    Don't worry about it.

NEMO
    Thanks. See ya later.

ROLAND
    Sure thing.

        (SERGEANT CONNOR hangs up the phone and returns it to his pocket.)

NEMO
    So she'll drop them off and you'll bring them to me?

SERGEANT CONNER
    As long as my cookies are in there too. Otherwise I'm eating them.

NEMO
    I'm pretty sure I'm the only one who can stomach them, but if that's what it comes down to you have my permission.

        (SERGEANT CONNOR leaves. NEMO reads a book from under his chair while ROLAND goes off stage, there is a woman's scream. ROLAND comes back upstairs with bloody hands and the tin. ROLAND cleans his hands and the tin with a bar towel before dashing off. A short time later SERGEANT CONNER returns to NEMO'S cell with the tin of cookies in which is hidden an eye.)

SERGEANT CONNER
    Nemo, here's your package. Thanks for the business. Let me know if you need anything else.

NEMO
    I'm sure I will. Thanks, Pete. Did you try one?

SERGEANT CONNER
    No, you said they were bad and they didn't look very appetizing. Besides, I already got what I wanted.

NEMO
    Fair enough, I'll keep an eye out for you.

(After SERGEANT CONNOR leaves again NEMO opens the tin and offers one to someone next to him. After they take a cookie (NEMO could choose to insist) he then digs out the eye...he may also then offer another cookie. NEMO places the tin under his chair out of the way and holds up the eye so everyone can see.)

NEMO
    Perfect.

(The lights go down and the audience is left in silence while NEMO gets up and goes off stage.)

ACT III

(The lights come up on RAPHAEL's office and SERGEANT CONNOR escorts NEMO back to the door. NEMO enters the office and RAPHAEL addresses him immediately.)

DR. ALEXANDER
        (Upset and angry)
Mr. Tumblety, thank you for coming.

NEMO
You said it was urgent.

DR. ALEXANDER
        (Still angry, but hopeful)
I received your message. Please tell me it isn't hers.

NEMO
(NEMO picks up a letter from RAPHAEL'S desk and reads it out loud.) Dear Dr. Alexander, I wanted you to look me in the eye when we talk, but since you've decided to send me away I made sure that you had an eye, one that you're sure to remember, to look into. Please let me know if there are any other parts that you want to keep. Sincerely, Nemo Tumblety. P.S. I'd suggest putting that in some formaldehyde or something. Pretty sure it'll start to smell soon, but you've probably got a little time since it was plucked fresh this morning. Yours, -N.
        (NEMO returns to addressing RAPHAEL directly.)
I'm pretty sure that spells out quite plainly whose eye it is, don't you?

DR. ALEXANDER
        (Distraught)
Nemo, there has to be something that you want. Something that I can give you to make you stop doing this. I want my little girl back.

NEMO
Look, you're a nice guy, but you're in the same boat as she is. The only trouble here is that I met her before I met you and I'm not really in a position to help you like I am her. There's really nothing to be done but let me set her free.

DR. ALEXANDER
        (Stopping)
Everyone has their price. Name yours and I'll pay it. I'll do anything.

NEMO
The thing is, Raph, I just sent you the note to show you there are no hard feelings. I know how sentimental people can be so I wanted you to have something to remember her by. When you look at it you'll know that she isn't trapped any more. You don't like it?

DR. ALEXANDER
No!

NEMO
Gee, I'm sorry, I could get you something else. You want me to get rid of it for you?

DR. ALEXANDER
Nemo, I believe I have to try to help you for her sake.
(Steeling himself)
So, let's talk. That's what you want, right? And if you can convince me that setting Alexi free is the right choice then I'll give you my permission.

NEMO
Really, you mean it?

DR. ALEXANDER
You must be honest with me. If you hold anything back I will not be able to say yes and you'll have to give Alexi back to me.

NEMO
I don't know about that last part.

DR. ALEXANDER
You said yourself that you needed her to ask and since she can't you need me to do it for her.

NEMO
(Considers)
I guess I did say that. OK, let's talk. I'm sure you'll come around eventually.

DR. ALEXANDER
OK, why don't we return to where we left off? You told me what got you started. Now tell me what makes you continue to do these things.

NEMO
To do that I'll have to tell you about Harriet Tubbs.

DR. ALEXANDER
Another person whom you helped to find freedom?

NEMO
    That is what we're here to talk about, isn't it?

DR. ALEXANDER
    Yes, fine, go on.

NEMO
    Harriet was a nice old broad. She'd lived a long, long time and she had some pretty debilitating pain.

DR. ALEXANDER
    Where did you meet her?

NEMO
    Where else? Inspiration Point. It's where I met all my friends.

DR. ALEXANDER
    Go on.

> *(NEMO walks to the bar while he talks and HARRIET joins him when appropriate. ROLAND is behind the bar and HARRIET is quite drunk.)*

NEMO
    She actually asked me to help her the very first time we met. I was sitting in the bar sipping whiskey and watching the people go through their routines when the old girl sat down at my table.

HARRIET
    Hey there, tall dark and handsome, you look pretty lonely all by yourself over here.

NEMO
    I'm fine, but I think that you might've had a little too much to drink.

HARRIET
    You know what? I think you might be right (hiccup), but you can probably forgive me a little bit of indulging.

NEMO
    You should know that you're a slave to the booze, but I guess there are worse things.

HARRIET
    It's the only way I can get away from the arthritis for just a little while.

NEMO
    But it's still there.

HARRIET
Oh, I know that, but for right now it's the least of my worries.

NEMO
So you're giving up one prison for another. You can't ever just be yourself. That must be pretty rough.

HARRIET
Not a lot I can do about my problems. That Kevorkian man up and died before I could get an appointment with him.

NEMO
The suicide doctor?

HARRIET
It probably wouldn't have worked anyway. It's so far away, but it's nice to think about, you know?

NEMO
I think I do. So you'd actually want to be free from these burdens?

HARRIET
If I could do it myself I'd be done already, but I can't squeeze the trigger and I can't bring myself to take the pills. I might fail.

NEMO
Well, I'm glad you sat down. Looks like fate guided you to me.

HARRIET
What do you mean?

NEMO
Here, let me get you another drink.

HARRIET
That's fine, I gotta use the ladies. I hope you're still here when I get back. Not many guys will talk to an old goat like me.

NEMO
I'll still be here.

> *(The lights go down and HARRIET and NEMO move to the kill room. HARRIET is bound to NEMO'S table when the lights come back up on the kill room.)*

NEMO

So, Harriet, how was the drink.

HARRIET
(Drowsy)
Where am I?

NEMO

This is where I bring my most important guests. You asked me to bring you here last night.

HARRIET

Oh, honestly, you're much too young for me. I don't think I would've...

NEMO

Ah, but you did. You were telling me about your troubles and I explained that you were always a prisoner, but only the warden had changed.

HARRIET

I remember a little, but that last drink was a doozy.

NEMO

Sorry about that. I had to be sure that you'd come home with me.

HARRIET

You drugged me?

NEMO

Just enough to convince you to stick to your guns, so to speak.

HARRIET
(sounding worried)
Well, I hope we had fun. I should be getting home now. I...

NEMO

You don't have to go back to jail. I'm here to help you make sure that your parole is permanent.

HARRIET

What do you mean?

NEMO

You said that you wanted to visit Dr. Kevorkian and you were sad that he died before you got the chance.

HARRIET

I suppose I might've said that.

NEMO

> Well, I'm not a doctor, but I can still get the job done.

HARRIET
> (Unsure)
> Yes, but I have responsibilities.

NEMO

> Just more shackles, Harriet, let me help you. You don't have to feel pain any more.

HARRIET
> (Considers)
> Will it hurt?

NEMO

> Not if you don't want it to. All you have to do is ask me to set you free and we can forgo all of the parts where I show you that it's what you really need.

HARRIET

> Well then, I guess I'd like you to set me free.

NEMO

> Oh, Harriet, I'm so glad. Are you comfortable?

HARRIET

> Yes, I suppose I am.

NEMO

> Harriet Tubbs, you are amazing to me. So few people know what they truly need and have the courage to pursue it. I've never been more proud.

HARRIET

> How are you going to do it?

NEMO

> Just like this...

>> (The lights fade as NEMO slowly pulls a scalpel along HARRIET'S neck. HARRIET screams wetly and then there is silence. When the lights come back up NEMO is in RAPHAEL'S office again and HARRIET is gone.)

NEMO

> You know doc, Harriet really made me understand that people know they want freedom more than anything and that I can help them achieve it.

DR. ALEXANDER
    What did you do to her?

NEMO
    Oh, that's right, there wouldn't be any reports. I took her skin.

DR. ALEXANDER
    Good heavens...

NEMO
    She stayed alive through most of the removal process. It helped that she was old and her skin was already pretty loose. I preserved Harriet and then I made leather from her skin. I actually donated several homemade footballs to a high school that didn't have enough money for new ones. Harriet was so happy.

DR. ALEXANDER
    The police never found the body.

NEMO
    No, Harriet is still in my possession. When I wasn't in prison I would look in on her from time to time. We still talk about the night we met at Inspiration Point and we laugh and laugh.

DR. ALEXANDER
    I think that our time is up.

NEMO
    So it is. Now that you know why I press on are you ready to let me help your family?

DR. ALEXANDER
    I don't think I understand what you do, Nemo. I'm simply not convinced.

NEMO
    That's too bad. I guess I'll be seeing you again then.

DR. ALEXANDER
    I thought we had a deal. I listen and if I'm not convinced then you let me have my Alexi back.

NEMO
    Oh, doc, you shouldn't make deals if you don't fully understand them. You're right, that's our deal, but you didn't include how long I would have to convince you. Don't worry though, since we're talking she's probably still alive. See you tomorrow.
            (NEMO gets up and opens the door to
            where SERGEANT CONNOR is waiting.)
                    (MORE)

NEMO (cont'd)
    I'm ready to go now Sergeant Conner.

        *(SERGEANT CONNOR escorts NEMO off stage and
        RAPHAEL addresses FRED on his phone.)*

DR. ALEXANDER
    Did you hear all of that?

FRED ABBERLINE
    Yeah, this guy is pretty sick.

DR. ALEXANDER
    And he has my daughter, Mr. Abberline. I need your
    help.

FRED
    It'll take me a little bit, but I'll see what I can
    find on Harriet. That might give you some leverage.

DR. ALEXANDER
    Thank you, Fred, I don't know what I'd do without you.

FRED
    You don't have to thank me, just make sure I get my
    money...

        (The lights go down)

25.

ACT IV

(NEMO enters RAPHAEL'S office again showing that it is a new day in some way. He begins to walk to the sofa, but stops when RAPHAEL tells him that he has a present for him.)

NEMO
    So round, three, eh, doc?

DR. ALEXANDER
    Yes, but this time I have something for you.

NEMO
    Interesting! I have something for you too, but you first, I love surprises.

DR. ALEXANDER
    Here.

(RAPHAEL pushes a case forward on his desk. NEMO opens the case and goes quiet with delight for a moment before proceeding.)

NEMO
    I can't wait to see what... what's this?

DR. ALEXANDER
    You don't recognize it?

NEMO
    Of course I do.

DR. ALEXANDER
    Then asking seems a little silly, doesn't it?

NEMO
    I only meant what I got you isn't half as nice as this.
        (NEMO removes a skinless, desiccated human arm-or just reaches into the case and pets the arm if a suitable human arm cannot be located.)
    Harriet and I haven't been together in a long time. Even just her arm makes me feel close to her again.

DR. ALEXANDER
    Yes, well, naturally that will have to stay here. The guards will not allow you to have it in your cell.

NEMO
    Do you think that we could be alone for just a little bit?

DR. ALEXANDER
Sergeant Conner is out in the lobby, Nemo. We are alone.

NEMO
No, I meant Harriet and me.

DR. ALEXANDER
I'm afraid not, in fact it's time to put her away.

(RAPHAEL shuts the case, or thrusts the arm back into the case closes it snapping the case closed with finality either way.)

NEMO
(Worried)
Now, wait a minute, doc. It's dark in there.

DR. ALEXANDER
I'm interested in your fascination with Harriet, Nemo.

NEMO
I don't like where this is going.

DR. ALEXANDER
Why is that?

NEMO
Because you're going to tell me that you'll give me Harriet back in exchange for your daughter and I just can't make that deal.

DR. ALEXANDER
Then I'm afraid that I have no choice but to turn Harriet's body over to the police.

NEMO
No! You can't do that. She's mine.

DR. ALEXANDER
And Alexi is mine.

NEMO
But Harriet is a free woman. Alexi isn't. It's apples and oranges.

DR. ALEXANDER
(Resigned sigh)
You said that you have something for me?

NEMO
(Irritated and moody)
Yeah, but I'm not so sure that you deserve it now.

DR. ALEXANDER
　　Just show me.

NEMO
　　Let's talk a little first and then we'll see.

DR. ALEXANDER
　　What do you want to talk about? I already know how and why you do these things. What more can I learn that will make you understand that I cannot be convinced to let you kill Alexi?

NEMO
　　Set her free...I asked myself that same question and I came up with the answer almost as quickly.

DR. ALEXANDER
　　Then tell me so that we can be done with all of this.

NEMO
　　On one of my last visits to Inspiration Point before I was arrested, I ran into an old friend of mine. A man named Arden Hetzler.

DR. ALEXANDER
　　You killed someone that you know?

NEMO
　　I realize you're not supposed to do that if you don't want to get caught, but as you may recall, Raphy, I wanted to get caught.

DR. ALEXANDER
　　Because you wanted to see me.

NEMO
　　That's half of the reason, but there was more to it than that. I needed to get caught.

DR. ALEXANDER
　　　　(Pondering)
　　Other than wanting to talk to me, why in God's name did you need to get caught?

NEMO
　　I can't set myself free; that would be wrong. I need someone to do it for me. When you and I are finished you are going to help me.

DR. ALEXANDER
　　　　(Skeptical)
　　You mean you want me to get you the death penalty?

NEMO
    That's it.

DR. ALEXANDER
    And that's all you want?

NEMO
    No, we have to finish this business with Alexi. When we are done you will testify that I was perfectly sane and knew what I was doing. You'll tell the judge to give me real freedom. It's what I deserve. You will do that for me.

DR. ALEXANDER
    Seeing you free would make me very happy.

NEMO
    Just don't do it yourself, okay Raphy? You wouldn't do very well in a prison of bricks and bars.

DR. ALEXANDER
    Fine. You were telling me about your friend Arden.

NEMO
    Right. I went to high school with the guy.

    (NEMO returns to the bar. ROLAND is behind the counter and ARDEN is at the table.)

NEMO
    Hey, don't I know you? Arden Hetle-something, right?

ARDEN
    Hetzler, yeah. Nemo "Rumbly" Tumblety. How've you been?

NEMO
    No one has called me that in years.

ARDEN
    Yeah, I guess you probably didn't keep in touch with too many people from school.

NEMO
    What makes you say that?

ARDEN
    Well, I mean after what happened.

NEMO
    Oh, right...

ARDEN
I heard you watched someone die. I'd need a heck of a lot of therapy to get over something like that. My therapist already takes enough of my money.

NEMO
Watching Susan die didn't bother me, but I do think about it sometimes. I'm pretty sure she got it easier than the rest of us.

ARDEN
Man that's messed up. She died.

NEMO
I suppose.

ARDEN
(Quickly changing the subject.)
So, uh, what have you been up to?

NEMO
I've been helping people escape slavery by showing them the path to freedom, you?

ARDEN
What?

NEMO
I'm kidding, I sell car parts.

ARDEN
(Suspicious)
Yeah, well, nice to catch up with you, I should really get going.

NEMO
Nonsense, let me buy you a drink. Who knows when we'll get the chance to see each other again.

ARDEN
I guess one more couldn't hurt.

NEMO
Yeah, I'm sure when you go it won't be because you drank too much. You look fit as a fiddle.

ARDEN
I spend a lot of time at the gym.

NEMO
Gym and therapy...how do you find the time?

ARDEN

>	Not much else to do I guess.

NEMO

>	Fair enough.

ARDEN

>	Hey, do you remember that English teacher that we both used to have?

NEMO

>	Mr. Schultz?

ARDEN

>	Yeah, I heard he died.

NEMO

>	I think the police found him with running shoes stuffed down his throat.

ARDEN

>	That's too bad.

NEMO

>	I guess, but he's free now just like he asked.

ARDEN

>	What do you mean?

NEMO

>	Nothing. Looks like the drinks are done. I'll go grab them.

>	*(NEMO goes to the bar and gets the drinks that ROLAND has poured, he drugs one of them and takes them back to the table giving ARDEN the drugged one.)*

NEMO

>	Here you go.

ARDEN

>	Thanks, all this talk about death has left me pretty thirsty.

NEMO

>	Well, drink up.

>	*(The lights go down and NEMO and ARDEN go to the kill room. When the lights come back up ARDEN is bound and NEMO is standing nearby. A syringe is on the table.)*

ARDEN
   Man I gotta quit drinking.

NEMO
   I don't think you have to worry about that any more.

ARDEN
   Nemo? What the heck happened last night?

NEMO
   You had a few too many, and I offered my place for you to sleep it off.

ARDEN
   And why am I strapped down?

NEMO
   To show you how important your freedom is, but I'm afraid we don't have time for all of that so I just need you to repeat after me and then I'll remove the straps and we can get on with what must be done.

ARDEN
   You're kinda scaring me. I'd like it if you took these straps off. I think I'm fine now.

NEMO
   No, you need to say, "I want you to set me free."

ARDEN
   Why?

NEMO
   Do you want me to take the straps off?

ARDEN
   Yes.

NEMO
   Then say it.

ARDEN
   Fine, I want you to set me free, Nemo.

NEMO
   Perfect.

     (NEMO takes the syringe and injects the contents into ARDEN'S neck.)

ARDEN
   What was that?

NEMO
> It's a paralytic. You see, Harriet screamed a lot when I took her skin off and I don't want you to have to experience the same thing. It'll trouble your soul.

ARDEN
> What the fffff...

NEMO
> Shhh, take it easy. It stops your vocal cords from vibrating. Here we go.
>
> *(The lights go down and there is only silence. When the lights come back up ARDEN is gone and NEMO is back on RAPHAEL'S sofa.)*

DR. ALEXANDER
> So what did you do to him?

NEMO
> I took his skin off and he didn't even scream. I'd learned a lot since Harriet.

DR. ALEXANDER
> Why the skin?

NEMO
> It's useful for all sorts of stuff. I'd like the people I help to know that their remains will be used for something that will give them purpose.

DR. ALEXANDER
> And how is Arden's story supposed to convince me to let you set Alexi free?

NEMO
> The guy was terrible, Dr. Alexander. He did awful things to girls and boys alike during high school.

DR. ALEXANDER
> Alexi is not a bad person.

NEMO
> No, she is not, but don't you want her to be safe from bad men?

DR. ALEXANDER
> More than anything.

NEMO
> Hey, that reminds me, I think you've been good. You can have your present now. Here, take it...

DR. ALEXANDER
   Nemo, if there is another piece of Alexi inside of this box so help me...

NEMO
   Just open it, open it.

   (RAPHAEL opens the box and turns grim.)

DR. ALEXANDER
   Nemo, this is Alexi's ear.

NEMO
   No.

DR. ALEXANDER
   Then whose ear is it?

NEMO
   Look, there's some hair there—brilliant red hair that belongs to an equally brilliant and stunningly beautiful woman.

DR. ALEXANDER
   (Distraught)
   Nemo, what have you done?

NEMO
   I was worried that you might make an effort to use your resources to find Harriet. So I had to find a way to protect her.

DR. ALEXANDER
   You have my wife.

NEMO
   Excellent deduction, Raph. I didn't want Harriet to get in the way of our deal. So let's just trade Harriet for your wife and then we can focus on Alexi next time.

DR. ALEXANDER
   Do I have any other choice?

NEMO
   No. I'll work out the finer points of the trade and communicate them to you later.

DR. ALEXANDER
   I think it's time for you to go.

NEMO
   See you tomorrow.

DR. ALEXANDER
    Sergeant, Mr. Tumblety is ready to go back to his cell.

    (With the previous line RAPHAEL and NEMO walk to the door to address SERGEANT CONNOR.)

SERGEANT CONNER
    Sure thing, doc. Let's go, Nemo.

    (After NEMO and SERGEANT CONNOR are gone RAPHAEL addresses FRED on the speaker phone.)

DR. ALEXANDER
    Mr. Abberline how could this have happened? You said you had someone watching my house.

FRED
    I did... I'll find out and call you back.

DR. ALEXANDER
    You do that. I'm not paying you so that my whole family can end up dead.

FRED
    We'd better just make the trade for now and we'll find another way to get this sleazeball.

DR. ALEXANDER.
    Get it done, Mr. Abberline, just get it done.

    (The lights go down.)

ACT V

> *(Again we show that time has passed and the lights come back up on RAPHAEL'S office. Another chair has been added behind the desk and both RAPHAEL and FRED stand behind the desk.)*

DR. ALEXANDER
> Fred, again, I can't thank you enough for getting Irena back safe.

FRED
> How's she doing?

DR. ALEXANDER
> A madman cut off her ear. What do you think?

FRED
> Yeah, right, well, you think you're ready for this?

DR. ALEXANDER
> Yes, of course I am. This man has to be stopped.

FRED
> Good.

DR. ALEXANDER
> I'd still like to know how he managed to get to Irena in the first place.

FRED
> We can't focus on that now. When does the guy get here?

DR. ALEXANDER
> He should be here with Sergeant Conner any minute now.

> *(KNOCK ON THE DOOR)*

DR. ALEXANDER
> Come in.

> *(NEMO enters and goes to his seat on the sofa before he notices FRED)*

NEMO
> Oh, hey, doc. I didn't realize that you had another patient in here. I can wait in the hall with Sergeant Conner.

DR. ALEXANDER
> No, Nemo, this is a friend of mine, Mr. Fred...(pause)...Johnson, I've asked him here to see if he can help both of us come to some amicable agreement.

NEMO
You're a shrink too?

FRED
No, I'm an investigator.

NEMO
Ah, so you're the guy who helped Raphael here find Harriet.

FRED
That's me.

(NEMO jumps up to shake FRED'S hand, but FRED declines.)

NEMO
Which means you helped get her back to me too. Thank you, sir, I really appreciate it.

FRED
Don't mention it.

DR. ALEXANDER
Gentlemen, please take a seat.

(They all sit. RAPHAEL and FRED behind the desk and NEMO on the sofa.)

NEMO
So, doc, what do you and... Fred was it? want to talk about today?

DR. ALEXANDER
Well, I thought that we could start with where you are holding my daughter.

NEMO
Oh, I'm not holding her anywhere.

FRED
Maybe not, but you've got help from someone on the outside who is.

NEMO
Then that person is holding on to Dr. Alexander's daughter. At best, I'm an accomplice.

FRED
But you do know who it is and where they are?

NEMO

I didn't say that either. Doc, did you bring me here to grill me or to help me to get through my problems because I think that we both have better things to do and Alexi probably can't afford to have you wasting time like this.

DR. ALEXANDER
(Shouting)
Just tell us where she is.

NEMO

Don't worry, I will. And I won't even take her skin. All you have to do is ask me to set her free.

DR. ALEXANDER
I don't wish for you to kill her.

NEMO

Doc, we've been over this. It's not killing. It's opening a door.

DR. ALEXANDER
You see what he does? I feel trapped and all he does is rebut every line of questioning.

NEMO

If you're feeling trapped, Dr. Alexander, I know someone who is an expert at helping people realize their freedom.

FRED

Let's try this way. You tell us where the girl is being kept and we'll see that you get a nice cell with a view for the rest of your life.

DR. ALEXANDER
He doesn't want that.

FRED

You don't?

NEMO

No. I want my freedom.

FRED

Well that's not going to happen. There's not a judge alive who is going to set you free.

NEMO

That is where you are wrong.

FRED
> Listening to you two on the phone was hard enough, but the two of you in person is enough to drive a man crazy.

NEMO
> The doc can help you with that problem. Well, at least he says he can. I think his plate is a bit full at the moment though. But more on point, shame on you, Dr. Alexander, letting someone listen in on our private talks without my permission. That's probably going to be pretty expensive for you.

DR. ALEXANDER
> What do you mean?

NEMO
> Well...
> (NEMO pauses and looks frustrated)
> do you mind if I walk around a little?

DR. ALEXANDER
> As long as you stay on that side of the desk.

(NEMO gets up and walks around stopping at the door when appropriate.)

NEMO
> The way I see it, Raph, you've given me another bargaining chip.

DR. ALEXANDER
> How do you figure?

NEMO
> Couldn't you lose your ability to practice if someone found out that you were letting private investigators listen to patient conversations?

DR. ALEXANDER
> It's a common practice.

NEMO
> Even when the patient doesn't know about it and the investigator in question isn't assigned to the patient's case, but is instead working for you?

DR. ALEXANDER
> I will deny it.

NEMO
> You would lie?

FRED
: And I'll back him up.

NEMO
: So I guess it's just the word of a crazy person who allegedly killed some people against the corrupt psychiatrist and his lackey. Does that sound about right?

DR. ALEXANDER
: If anyone is corrupt in this room, Mr. Tumblety, it's you.

NEMO
: That is an interesting point of view. This is a curious door. I've come through it so many times and I never noticed it really. What is it, mahogany?

DR. ALEXANDER
: It's oak, but that doesn't really matter. We are talking about freeing my daughter. You have to let her go.

NEMO
: No...
    (NEMO knocks on the door three times and becomes excited)
I suppose the wood doesn't really matter.

FRED
: Listen, this'll all be a lot easier if you tell us where Alexi is before you get yourself in any more trouble.

NEMO
: You know, I think maybe you are right.

FRED
:   (Surprised)
I am?

DR. ALEXANDER
:   (At the same time also surprised)
He is?

NEMO
: Yup. You'll find the girl at 213 Elmwood Drive. It's a big house owned by a doctor.

FRED
:   (FRED takes out his phone and dialing)
Well, see, that wasn't so hard.

NEMO
> (Chuckles)
> This has really been fun, hasn't it? But I guess we won't be having any more sessions, huh, doc?

DR. ALEXANDER
> No, we most certainly will not. I'll see you hang for this.

NEMO
> I don't think that they hang people anymore, doc, but I'm sure they'll find a proper way to thank me for my time with you.

FRED
> This is Fredrick Abberline. Yeah, she's at 213 Elmwood Drive. There's a suspect there too. Make sure you take plenty of guys with you. OK, thanks.

(FRED puts his phone back in his pocket.)

FRED
> The officers are on their way.

NEMO
> Whatever happens next, doc, I hope that someday you'll be able to look back on all of this fondly.

(Silence. The lights go down and more time passes. RAPHAEL enters his office alone when the lights come back up. He searches his desk drawers until he finds his journal and a pen and then sits down to write. As he writes he speaks his next line.)

DR. ALEXANDER
> It's been several months since I last had Nemo Tumblety in my office and the memory of his words still haunts me. I know now that those words were not his own, but I hope that we do not meet again. It has taken me some time to come to grips with what I now know to be true. Over these last few months during Sergeant Conner's trial I learned that Nemo was a pawn in a game played by sick men. They killed my darling Alexi. Sergeant Connor and his accomplice Roland Tarrance, the real culprits, now await their fates, and while Nemo is innocent of the crimes, I...

(FRED knocks on the door and enters after RAPHAEL'S NEXT LINE)

DR. ALEXANDER
> Come in...

FRED
       Evening, Raph, I thought I'd stop by and see how you're
       doing since you ducked out of the courthouse pretty
       quickly this afternoon.

DR. ALEXANDER
       I've just been having a hard time with all of this, but
       I'm glad that Alexi's killers will be punished. Still,
       it's all hard to believe that none of what Nemo said
       were his own words.

FRED
       Yeah, that guy was pretty spooky. Still, Roland and
       Conner confessed and there was so much evidence at
       Inspiration Point—pictures, murder weapons, the whole
       thing. You helped catch a serial killer.

DR. ALEXANDER
       I wasn't fast enough though, they still killed Alexi.

FRED
       It's unfortunate, Raphael, but we got the guys
       responsible and they won't hurt anybody else.

DR. ALEXANDER
       There are still some things about Nemo that bother me.

FRED
       Like what?

DR. ALEXANDER
       I know that Conner told Nemo what to say, but when they
       found Alexi she hadn't been gone long. How did Nemo
       know that it was time to give us the address? There
       must have been some kind of signal.

FRED
       The text message to order the guy to do it came from
       Conner's phone. Apparently, he ordered Nemo to knock
       on the door to tell him to send it once you said that
       you wanted him to free your daughter.

DR. ALEXANDER
       I didn't say that.

FRED
       Well, you said that you wanted him to let her go right
       after mentioning her freedom.

DR. ALEXANDER
       That's not what I meant.

FRED
   It was close enough for a crazy person.

DR. ALEXANDER
   And what about this text message? All it said was, "It's time for more cookies."

FRED
   Sergeant Connor and Roland must have worked out some kind of code before they sent Nemo into your office.

DR. ALEXANDER
   I just can't shake the feeling that Nemo was involved in some way.

FRED
   Well, according to the Judge, he's innocent. He was controlled by Conner the whole time.

DR. ALEXANDER
   I know. And I'm working on accepting that it's the truth. Nemo seemed so sincere.

FRED
   He was a good actor. I still don't think that guy's quite right in the head. I mean, obviously they convicted him with some evidence the first time.

DR. ALEXANDER
   I suppose. That's what bothers me. Why'd they let him go?

FRED
   There isn't anything you can do, but move on. The cop confessed and fingered his accomplice. Nemo has been released and he's going to get quite a settlement for the wrongful imprisonment.

DR. ALEXANDER
   I suppose I should be glad that the right people are in prison and those responsible are going to be punished. It's just so hard to reconcile.

FRED
   I understand, but you can't dwell on it. You have to live your life otherwise you'll wind up doing exactly what Conner tells his victims.

DR. ALEXANDER
   Yes, I suppose you're right, I don't want to make a prison for myself and make Alexi's death meaningless. I have to go on for her.

(The lights go down and come back up on the bar. SEAMUS is now bartender. NEMO sits across the table from MRS. CONNOR.)

NEMO
So anyway, Mrs. Conner, that's what I think. You're a brave woman and you don't need someone like Peter in your life any more.

MRS. CONNOR
You've been so kind to me, Mr. Tumblety. I'm so sorry that you spent time in that awful place for what my husband did. I'm glad that you invited me here. I'd hate to think that you blame our whole family for Peter's mistakes.

NEMO
Yeah, I'm so sorry that he put you through all of this, you seem nice.

MRS. CONNOR
I never would have thought him capable of such terrible things...

NEMO
Peter was a prisoner before his trial. He gambled all of your money away. What's worse is that he didn't just trap himself. He brought you with him.

MRS. CONNOR
(Sobbing)
I wish that I could have mustered the courage to stop him. I knew something was wrong.

NEMO
I helped him and now he'll know freedom soon. It's because of his honesty that I can continue my work. You should remember that he was brave when it mattered.

(MRS CONNOR takes out a handkerchief and dries her eyes.)

MRS. CONNOR
You are too kind, but you're right. He needs me by his side now more than ever. I should go see him.

NEMO
When I spoke to him he insisted that I tell you to stay away. He was worried about your safety and told me you'd get along fine without my help, but I couldn't bear to leave you in the cage he made for you. Hey, you've been listening to me blather for the better part of an hour now. Can I get you a drink?

Afterword...

When I sat down to pen the original radio drama that would later be transformed into this play I wasn't exactly sure what would happen. I looked through all of my usual sources for the spark of an idea, but nothing occurred to me so I used Google to look for inspirational pictures. As you might imagine the result were a lot of, often humorous, encouraging and inspirational photos. I was sickened by the level of optimism that my laptop was exuding, but I pressed on.

Finally I came to the really interesting stuff. The first photo that caught my attention was a bridge that disappeared into a dark wood. Now we were on to something dark and sinister amid all of the despicable cheer and words of wisdom that are probably really helpful to people who need them. My faith restored that I might find something to put me on the right track I scrolled onward looking for more images like the bridge into darkness.

Gandhi, President Obama, several adorable (but ultimately undesirable) kittens and even Al Gore breathing fire didn't have as much impact on the picture that next drew my attention. The image was a black and white photo of a sign that was rusty and dented with the words INSPIRATION POINT embossed in plain, uninteresting black letters.

I felt a strange an ominous mood wash over me as I looked at the sign and knew that was going to be the title of whatever it was that I was going to write. There, that was done. I had a title page. Not a whole lot of substance there, but I'm a writer so I should be able to find a few things in my brain to entertain the masses, right?

I chose Nemo because it means nobody and Tumblety in homage to one of the many folks thought to have been Jack the Ripper. As I started to write I could hear his voice in my head. Slow, almost prayerful, as he began to describe to his friend, Raphael Alexander (whose name means healer—though apparently not a very good one), just exactly how happy it made him to watch his victims die. Nemo was clearly disturbed (which says something, probably, about my character, but we're not talking about that right now...).

Nemo tells us his vision. There is a way to get away from all of the bindings that we let the world tie us down with, but only if we are brave and accepting of the truth. The only way not to be a slave to fashion, money, power, greed, anger, rage or the sea of other perfectly normal human emotions is to die. I mean it's perfectly reasonable, isn't it? We can't figure out the meaning of life so wouldn't it just be easier not to participate?

Most folks, Dr. Alexander included, rebel against this notion. It's better to have lived and tried to find the meaning of life than to have never lived at all, or something like that. These people have bought into the life lessons taught to us by the myriad of fictional characters who have wished that they had never been born only to be shown just how terrible the world would be if they had never existed. They are shown sad people and often apocalyptic changes that are the result of them refusing to leave the safety of their mother's womb when in truth, most people don't amount to more than a life well lived or worse a life flittered away on frivolous things.

Let us be cautious here. I'm not suggesting that the only way for you to escape is to end your life. On the contrary, I'm suggesting that you need to join the people who either already have a destiny or have the will to shape their own future into something that will leave behind a legacy. You don't have to die to escape those things to which most people succumb, but you do have to struggle and work hard to overcome all of the difficulties that life will find to put in your way when you try to succeed. The problem is not that people can't succeed and avoid being a slave to one aspect of life or another, but rather that they choose to allow their lives to be ruled by these things.

As I pressed on through the play I knew that Nemo had to be able to get out of prison and so I sent him the security guard and Inspector Aberline (who probably came closer than anyone else to actually catching Jack the Ripper—yes, I have a small serial killer crush, but he's dead and not killing anyone any more so it's healthy). These two gave Nemo the tools to escape his real world confinement by providing a scapegoat and a potential legal loophole for Nemo's defense attorney to use to get him off the hook (or the security guard is really responsible and Nemo really was just a patsy he was using to do his dirty work and he got out on the same technicality that the play suggests—I'm honestly not going to tell you how I think it goes because I think that takes some of the fun out of the story). Sure, the ending makes Nemo sound like he's back to his old tricks, but maybe he honestly just wants to buy a grieving widow a drink. Did you stop for a moment to consider that possibility before this moment? I thought not.

    Now Nemo (or Sergeant Conner) had everything that he needed to get into jail, get permission to kill Raphael's daughter (excuse me…to set her free) and get out again so that he could get back to work. As the rest of the story happens we experience the true depths of the killer's madness (or absolute sanity depending on your point of view—we're not here to judge you either way). He skins his victims, donates parts of them to depraved children and keeps the rest to help assuage his loneliness. He gets better at his job with each successive kill and further refines his mission statement while uncovering new prisons that terrify him into continuing to do what he must.

    I was inspired by *Silence of the Lambs*, *Saw* and *The Shining* throughout the creative process and I owe quite a lot to the folks who made those works of fiction so fantastic that they caught my attention and gave me the points of reference necessary to create my own story. I extend my heartfelt thanks and interminable gratitude for their efforts and inspiration.

    After we recorded the radio drama version (which you can listen to at **www.StrobieStudios.com**) I teamed up with my friend and business partner Kevin Brubaker to transform it into the play that you have just witnessed (in some form or another) and we have plans, with assistance from Kevin's ever delightful wife, Deb Brubaker, to turn Inspiration Point into an independent film in the near future. You can learn more about all of the things that we do by visiting the website that I mentioned above or **www.jumpstartmovie.com**.

Best wishes,
Michael R. Helgens
Cedar Rapids, IA - 2014

www.ingramcontent.com/pod-product-compliance
Lightning Source LLC
Chambersburg PA
CBHW081456060426
42444CB00037BA/3329